W9-AYF-736

PRIMARY SOURCES OF
FAMOUS PEOPLE IN AMERICAN HISTORY™

WYATT EARP

LAWMAN OF THE AMERICAN WEST

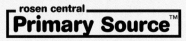

MAGDALENA ALAGNA

rosen central
Primary Source™
The Rosen Publishing Group, Inc., New York

Published in 2004 by The Rosen Publishing Group, Inc.
29 East 21st Street, New York, NY 10010

Library of Congress Cataloging-in-Publication Data

Alagna, Magdalena.
Wyatt Earp : lawman of the American West / by Magdalena Alagna.
    v. cm. — (Primary sources of famous people in American history)
Includes bibliographical references and index.
Contents: The early years—Indian territory—Cowboys and ranchers—The O.K. Corral —The last years.
ISBN 0-8239-4123-X (lib. bdg.)
ISBN 0-8239-4195-7 (pbk.)
6-pack ISBN 0-8239-4322-4
1. Earp, Wyatt, 1848–1929—Juvenile literature. 2. Peace officers—Southwest, New— Biography—Juvenile literature. 3. United States marshals—Southwest, New—Biography— Juvenile literature. 4. Tombstone (Ariz.)—History—Juvenile literature. 5. Southwest, New— Biography—Juvenile literature. [1. Earp, Wyatt, 1848–1929. 2. Peace officers.]
I. Title. II. Series.
F786.E18A4 2003
978'.02'092—dc21

2002155706

Manufactured in the United States of America

Photo credits: cover, pp. 5, 15, 24, 27 courtesy Arizona Historical Society/Tucson; p. 4 Library of Congress Prints and Photographs Division, HABS, IOWA, 63-PEL,3-1; p. 6 Steve Gatto; p. 7 Library of Congress Geography and Map Division; p. 8 National Archives and Records Administration, Old Military and Civil Records; p. 9 Library of Congress Prints and Photographs Division; p. 11 Kansas State Historical Society; p. 11 (inset) Western History Collections, University of Oklahoma Libraries; p. 12 © Corbis; p. 13 © John Van Hasselt/Corbis Sygma; pp. 17 (Joseph Collier, C-107), 18 (X-150) Denver Public Library, Western History Collection; p. 19 Hassel © collection of the New-York Historical Society NYHS #40747; p. 21 Culver Pictures; p. 23 © Bowers Museum of Cultural Art/Corbis; p. 25 Camilius S. Fly © collection of the New-York Historical Society NYHS #40746; p. 28 photo by Dick George; p. 29 courtesy of Stephen and Marge Elliot, Tombstone Western Heritage Museum.

Designer: Thomas Forget; Photo Researcher: Rebecca Anguin-Cohen

CONTENTS

1   EARLY YEARS

Wyatt Earp was born on March 19, 1848. In 1864, the Earp family led a wagon train to California. Wyatt was sixteen years old. They traveled on the Oregon Trail. Wyatt worked on a farm and also in a restaurant as a waiter. Wyatt grew to be about six feet tall. That was tall for those days.

Wyatt Earp lived in this house in Iowa until the age of sixteen. His father was a merchant. His mother raised the children.

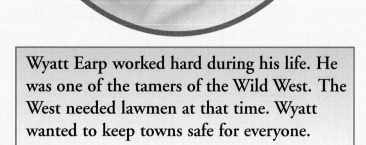

Wyatt Earp worked hard during his life. He was one of the tamers of the Wild West. The West needed lawmen at that time. Wyatt wanted to keep towns safe for everyone.

Wyatt Earp married Rilla Sutherland on January 24, 1870. He became the constable in Lamar, Missouri. Rilla died of an illness, and Wyatt left Lamar. He went to Arkansas and then to Indian Territory. Today this land is in Oklahoma. Wyatt met Bat Masterson in 1871 in Indian Territory. The two men would be good friends for the rest of their lives.

> This document is the oath of office Earp took for constable of Lamar, Missouri. An oath demands that laws must be upheld. Earp took this oath seriously.

State of Missouri
County of Barton

I, Wyatt S Earp do solemnly swear that I will to the best of my skill and ability, diligently, and faithfully without partiality or prejudice discharge the duties of Constable within and for Lamar Township, Barton County, Missouri

Wyatt S. Earp

Subscribed and sworn to before me this 24th day of November 1869

Clerk

Wyatt moved from Lamar, Missouri, after his wife died. He decided to try his skills in Indian Territory. These lands were not yet settled by a state government.

2   INDIAN TERRITORY

There were many kinds of people in Indian Territory. There were many native peoples and cowboys. Cowboys were the men who drove cattle through the small towns called cattle towns. These towns were wild places. Wyatt Earp became a lawman called a peace officer. He helped to keep such towns safe for those who lived there.

The United States government signed many treaties with Native Americans. These treaties forced them to move off eastern lands. Indian Territory held thousands of Native Americans.

AMERICAN HOMESTEAD SPRING.

Homesteaders shared the land with Native Americans in the West. In western towns, many different people lived near each other. It was Wyatt's job to keep the peace.

In 1876, he met John Henry "Doc" Holliday. Doc was a dentist. Doc also liked to gamble. He spent a lot of time playing cards. Doc Holliday had a lung illness called tuberculosis. In 1876, Wyatt became a deputy marshal in Dodge City, Kansas.

DID YOU KNOW?

Doc Holliday was trained as a dentist in Philadelphia. Being a dentist was a good job for that time in history. Many people had bad teeth then.

Wyatt Earp lived in Dodge City, Kansas, for three years. He was the town's lawman. Doc Holliday *(inset)* was Wyatt's friend. Wyatt often used Doc as a deputy when keeping the peace.

By 1879, the cattle towns had become poor. Most no longer wanted to pay peace officers. In the summer of 1879, Wyatt got a letter from his brother, Virgil. He told Wyatt to come to Tombstone, Arizona. Virgil was the deputy marshal there. Wyatt and his other brother, Morgan, moved to Tombstone. Doc Holliday and his girlfriend went, too.

Peace officers were needed badly in western towns. Cowboys often fought each other in town.

Tombstone, Arizona, was a small desert town. It was a town that served ranchers and the cowboys working the ranches.

3 COWBOYS AND RANCHERS

Tombstone, Arizona, was a silver mining town. Wyatt Earp became deputy sheriff. His job was to keep the peace in town. At first there were not many fights in town. Then things changed for the cowboys. They began to lose their work on the ranches.

NAMING TOMBSTONE, ARIZONA

Ed Schieffelin wanted to find something in the Arizona Territory. People said he would find his tombstone there. He found a silver mine, got rich, and founded Tombstone, Arizona.

Cattle drives used many cowboys to bring cattle from one ranch to another. Trains began to do this job in the 1870s, and cowboys started to lose their jobs.

COL. O. W. WHEELER'S HERD, EN ROUTE FOR KANSAS PACIFIC RAILWAY, IN 1867.

Ranchers now did many jobs the cowboys used to do. The cowboys had to find other ways to make money. Many stole cattle and sold them. Their leader was Curly Bill Brocius. Cowboys who stole cattle were called rustlers. The cowboys sold their stolen cattle to other ranchers.

DID YOU KNOW?

Doc Holliday made the cowboys mad because he beat them at cards. Wyatt stood by his friend, but that made the cowboys hate Wyatt even more.

16

Cattle rustlers stole cattle from large herds. It could take many days before a rancher discovered the missing animals. By then the rustlers would have sold the cattle for cash.

Ranchers sold the cattle to the citizens of Tombstone. In 1880, someone stole six mules. Virgil, Morgan, and Wyatt went to the McLaury ranch. There they found good clues to prove that the McLaury family had the mules. The family said they would return the mules. They lied. The mules were not returned.

Mules were important work animals for ranchers. Stealing them was a serious crime. Rustling was just one crime that Wyatt and his deputies had to deal with.

Tom McLaury was a known cattle rustler in the
Tombstone area. Wyatt Earp had many run-ins with the
McLaury family.

4 THE O.K. CORRAL

On October 26, 1881, things boiled over between the Earps, the cowboys, and the ranchers. Virgil ordered the cowboys to leave town. The cowboys went to get their horses at the O.K. Corral, but they did not leave. They stayed in town, waving their guns and making threats against the Earp brothers.

A BAD SHERIFF

The sheriff of Tombstone was John Behan. He was friendly with the cowboys and the ranchers. He did not stop the cowboys from stealing cattle.

This photo shows the entrance to the O.K. Corral. There is not a lot of space for a gunfight between nearly a dozen people. The smoke from the gunfire quickly blinded the fighters.

21

The cowboys' threats led to a shootout. Virgil, Wyatt, and Morgan Earp, along with Doc Holliday were on one side. The five cowboys from the McLaury and Clanton families, and Sheriff John Behan, were on the other side. Virgil told the cowboys to put down their guns. In a moment, everything became confused.

MARSHALS AND SHERIFFS

What was the difference between a marshal and a sheriff? A marshal dealt with crimes inside a town. A sheriff dealt with crimes outside a town.

This drawing shows how the gunfight might have happened. The Earps stood outside the gate. The cowboys were getting their horses inside the corral.

Wyatt fired his gun just as a shot rang out from the cowboy side. Suddenly everyone was shooting and shouting. Only Wyatt did not get shot during the gunfight.

Sheriff Behan wanted to arrest the Earps. They refused to go to jail. The story about the shootout ran in papers across the United States. The legend of the O.K. Corral was born.

Here is a photograph of the three dead cowboys from the Clanton gang. Tom and Frank McLaury are left and center. Billy Clanton lies in the far right casket.

Joseph "Ike" Clanton escaped from the O.K. Corral during the shooting. He swore revenge upon the Earps. Two months later, the fighting started again.

5 AFTER THE GUNFIGHT

The fighting did not stop at the O.K. Corral. On December 28, 1881, Virgil was ambushed. He was hurt, but lived. Wyatt wanted Virgil to leave town. At the train station, there were men with shotguns waiting for Virgil. Another shootout took place. Some of the men with shotguns were killed. People blamed the Earps.

DID YOU KNOW?

Doc Holliday died in 1885. His last words were "That's funny." He might have said this because he died in bed instead of in one of the many gun battles he had.

Wyatt Earp owned part of the Oriental Saloon, pictured here.
Virgil Earp was shot outside the saloon in December 1881.

Wyatt spent the rest of his life in the West. He lived mostly in California. In the early 1900s, he met many Hollywood actors. He hoped that someday they would make a movie about the O.K. Corral. Wyatt died in Los Angeles, California, on January 13, 1929. Many years after his death, three movies were made about Wyatt.

Wyatt Earp is remembered by this tombstone in California. His second wife, Josephine, was buried by his side. The mystery around the gunfight at the O.K. Corral was never solved. Wyatt took it with him to the grave.

Hollywood liked the story of the gunfight at the O.K. Corral. Wyatt knew many actors in Hollywood in his later years. This photo shows him at the age of 75.

Courtesy of Stephen and Marge Elliot, Tombstone Western Heritage Museum

TIMELINE

1848—Wyatt Earp is born.

1868—Wyatt Earp works on the railroad in Wyoming, then works at his father's restaurant in Missouri.

1871—Rilla dies. Wyatt goes to live in Indian Territory.

1876—Wyatt Earp is deputy marshal in Dodge City, Kansas.

1881—The shootout takes place at the O.K. Corral. Virgil Earp is shot; his arm is crippled.

1887—Doc Holliday dies in bed in Colorado.

1929—Wyatt Earp dies in Los Angeles, California.

1864—The Earp family goes on a wagon train to settle in California.

1870—Wyatt Earp marries Rilla Sutherland. He is elected constable of Lamar, Missouri.

1874—Wyatt Earp is a policeman in Wichita, Kansas.

1879—Wyatt Earp is deputy sheriff in Tombstone, Arizona.

1882—Morgan Earp is killed.

1900—Warren Earp is killed.

GLOSSARY

ambushed (AM-bushd) Attacked by surprise from a hiding place.

confusing (kun-FYOOZ-ing) Hard to understand.

constable (KON-stuh-bul) A minor court officer, sometimes the equal of a policeman.

corral (kuh-RAL) A fenced area that holds horses, cattle, or other animals.

deputy marshal (DEP-yoo-tee MAR-shul) A law officer who helps another law officer, a second in command.

legend (LEH-jend) A story that has been passed down.

Oregon Trail (OR-eh-gon TRAYL) A path that many settlers took to California.

outlaws (OWT-lawz) People who break the law.

ranchers (RANCH-erz) People who work on large farms to raise cattle.

rustlers (RUHSS-uh-luhrs) People who steal horses or cattle.

territory (TER-ih-tor-ee) A piece of land.

threats (THRETS) Warnings people make to those they want to harm.

wagon train (WAG-un TRAYN) A group of wagons.

WEB SITES

Due to the changing nature of Internet links, the Rosen Publishing Group, Inc., has developed an online list of Web sites related to the subject of this book. This site is updated regularly. Please use this link to access the list:

http://www.rosenlinks.com/fpah/wear

PRIMARY SOURCE IMAGE LIST

Page 4: Photograph of Earp home in Pella, Iowa. It is currently housed at the Library of Congress, Washington, D.C.

Page 5: Photo of Wyatt Earp, 1886. It is currently housed at the Historical Society, Tucson, Arizona.

Page 7: Hand-colored map of Indian Territory, 1889. It is currently housed at the Library of Congress, Washington, D.C.

Page 8: Treaty between Six Nations and the United States, 1784. It is currently housed at the National Archives, Washington, D.C.

Page 9: Hand-colored lithograph titled *American Homesteader Spring* by Currier & Ives, 1869. It is currently housed at the Library of Congress, Washington, D.C.

Page 11 (large photo): Photograph of Front Street in Dodge City, Kansas, circa 1879. It is currently housed at the Kansas State Historical Society, Topeka, Kansas.

Page 11 (inset): Photograph of Doc Holliday, circa 1885. It is currently housed at the Western History Collections, University of Oklahoma Libraries, Tulsa, Oklahoma.

INDEX

ABOUT THE AUTHOR

Magdalena Alagna is an author and editor living in New York City.